Secrets
of
Meditation

J. Donald Walters

ISBN 1-56589-739-0
10 9 8 7 6 5 4 3 2 1

Photographs: J. Donald Walters
Designed by Christine Starner Schuppe
Crystal Clarity Design

Manufactured in China

Crystal Clarity, Publishers
14618 Tyler Foote Road
Nevada City, CA 95959
1-800-424-1055
http://www.consciousnet.com/CrystalClarity

A seed thought is offered for every day of the month. Begin a day at the appropriate date. Repeat the saying several times: first out loud, then softly, then in a whisper, and then only mentally. With each repetition, allow the words to become absorbed ever more deeply into your subconscious.

Thus, gradually, you will acquire a complete understanding of each day's thought. At this point, indeed, the truths set forth here will have become your own.

Keep the book open at the pertinent page throughout the day. Refer to it occasionally during moments of leisure. Relate the saying as often as possible to real situations in your life.

Then at night, before you go to bed, repeat the thought several times more. While falling asleep, carry the words into your subconscious, absorbing their positive influence into your whole being. Let it become thereby an integral part of your normal consciousness.

DAY ONE

The secret of meditation
is relinquishing
outward attachments,
and affirming
divine freedom within.

The secret of meditation
is sitting upright
with a straight spine;
feeling that your strength
emanates from your spine
rather than from the muscles
of your body.

DAY THREE

The secret of meditation
is holding your body
perfectly still;
gradually freeing yourself
from the compulsion
to move.

DAY FOUR

The secret of meditation
is deep relaxation:
Inhale, tense the body;
throw the breath out and relax.
Release into the
surrounding atmosphere,
like wisps of vapor,
any lingering eddies
of tension that you feel.

DAY FIVE

The secret of meditation
is to feel space
in the body, and gradually
expand that feeling
from the body outward,
into infinite space.

DAY SIX

The secret of meditation
is to focus your gaze
and attention
at the Christ center
between the eyebrows —
the seat of ecstasy in the body.

DAY SEVEN

The secret of meditation
is to pray with deep faith —
not as an outsider to heaven,
but as one whose true,
eternal home is heaven.

DAY EIGHT

The secret of meditation
is singing to God,
out loud or silently,
to awaken devotion
in the heart.

DAY NINE

The secret of meditation
is loving God
in whatever form you hold
especially dear, and praying,
"God — my Father,
Mother, dearest Friend —
I am Thine forever:
Thine alone!"

DAY TEN

The secret of meditation
is offering gifts of love
upward from your heart
to the Christ center
between the eyebrows,
like the flames in
an all-purifying fire.

DAY ELEVEN

The secret of meditation
is dwelling on the thought
of great saints,
past and present,
who have known God;
attuning your
consciousness to theirs.

DAY TWELVE

The secret of meditation
is radiating blessings
from your heart
outward to
all the world.

DAY THIRTEEN

The secret of meditation
is putting resolutely aside
every plan, every project,
and focusing on the moment.
(The world will be there still,
when you finish your meditation!)

DAY FOURTEEN

The secret of meditation
is to enter instantly
into the silence within,
and not waste precious time
in mental wandering.

DAY FIFTEEN

The secret of meditation
is to send any vagrant thoughts
in your mind soaring,
like a flock of birds,
upward through skies of
Infinity until they disappear
in the blue distance.

DAY SIXTEEN

The secret of meditation
is releasing yourself
from the limitations
of body and ego;
identifying yourself
with Infinity.

DAY SEVENTEEN

The secret of meditation
is to visualize God
in one of His eternal aspects —
as infinite light, cosmic sound,
eternal peace, love, or joy;
seek to unite yourself
with Him in that aspect.

DAY EIGHTEEN

The secret of meditation
is affirming contentment,
rather than expecting
God to do all the work
of bringing you out of darkness
into His infinite light and joy.

DAY NINETEEN

The secret of meditation
is dwelling on the thought
of God's love for you,
and destroying
any lingering doubts
in a bonfire of devotion.

DAY TWENTY

The secret of meditation
is one-pointed
concentration;
absorption in
the peace within.

DAY TWENTY-ONE

The secret of meditation
is receptivity to the
flow of God's grace,
in full awareness
that God's power alone
can liberate the soul.

DAY TWENTY-TWO

The secret of meditation
is offering yourself up
wholly to the Lord,
holding nothing back.

DAY TWENTY-THREE

The secret of meditation
is visualizing your breath
as a flow of energy in the spine,
upward with inhalation,
and downward with exhalation,
until the flow
seems a mighty river.

DAY TWENTY-FOUR

The secret of meditation
is to visualize
the energy in the spine
rising in joyful aspiration
toward the point
between the eyebrows.

DAY TWENTY-FIVE

The secret of meditation
is listening intently
to any sounds you hear
in the inner ear;
becoming
absorbed in them.

DAY TWENTY-SIX

The secret of meditation
is visualizing yourself
seated at the heart of eternity;
sending rays of divine love
outward from your center
to all the universe.

DAY TWENTY-SEVEN

The secret of meditation
is steadfastness:
For the more you meditate,
the more you
will want to meditate,
but the less you meditate,
the less will you find
meditation attractive.

DAY TWENTY-EIGHT

The secret of meditation
is affirming
that you already
are those high truths
towards which you aspire:
inner peace, divine love,
and perfect joy.

DAY TWENTY-NINE

The secret of meditation
is unifying your
inner and outer life:
offering every problem
up for resolution
to the peace within;
allowing that peace to infuse
your outward activities.

DAY THIRTY

The secret of meditation
is to keep your
concentration positive,
and not meditate
to the point of fatigue
or boredom.

DAY THIRTY-ONE

The secret of meditation
is seeing God
as the sole Doer,
and seeking His guidance
in everything you do.

Other Books in the Secrets Series
by J. Donald Walters

Secrets of Love
Secrets of Friendship
Secrets of Happiness
Secrets for Men
Secrets for Women
Secrets of Success
Secrets of Prosperity
Secrets of Leadership
Secrets of Winning People
Secrets of Inner Peace
Secrets of Self-Acceptance
Secrets of Emotional Healing
Secrets of Radiant Health and Well-Being

(for children)
Life's Little Secrets
Little Secrets of Success
Little Secrets of Happiness
Little Secrets of Friendship